CW01513033

Original title:
Fragments of the Eternal Cosmos

Copyright © 2025 Swan Charm
All rights reserved.

Author: Kene Elistrand
ISBN HARDBACK: 978-1-80561-413-5
ISBN PAPERBACK: 978-1-80561-974-1

Ethereal Glimmers

In twilight's grasp, the shadows dance,
Whispers of light in a fleeting trance.
Stars that twinkle, a gentle sway,
Guiding lost souls on their way.

A soft embrace, the night unfolds,
Tales of wonder, softly told.
Dreams like paper, fragile and bright,
Carried away on wings of night.

Shadows of the Cosmos

Where darkness reigns, the secrets lie,
In the hush of space, beneath the sky.
Galaxies swirl in a cosmic waltz,
Time and matter, forever at fault.

Nebulas breathe with colors so deep,
Awakening wonders from the cosmic sleep.
Echoes of stars, both old and new,
Crafting stories of me and you.

Veils of Starlight

Through gossamer threads, the starlight flows,
Kissing the earth with a gentle glow.
A symphony played on celestial strings,
Awakening dreams that the night always brings.

Moonlight whispers tales of old,
Of journeys taken, of hearts consoled.
Each gleaming spark a beacon of hope,
Uniting all wandering souls to cope.

The Language of Galaxies

In silent whispers, the stars converse,
Crafting a tale, the universe's verse.
Frequencies echo through the vast unknown,
Connecting hearts to the seeds they've sown.

Comets streak like thoughts in flight,
Painting the void throughout the night.
The language spoken in silence profound,
In each twinkling star, our answers are found.

A Pocket of Stars

In the hush of night, I find,
A pocket of stars, softly aligned.
Whispers of dreams float in the air,
Guiding lost hearts with tender care.

They shimmer brightly, stories untold,
Of wishes made and secrets of old.
Each twinkle a promise, a light in the dark,
Igniting the heavens with a hopeful spark.

I reach for the glow, a hand stretched wide,
Embracing the magic that lives inside.
In this celestial dance, I lose my fear,
For in every starlight, love draws near.

Time fades away, just like the dawn,
But the pocket of stars whispers on.
In every heartbeat, they softly hum,
Reminding me always that I am never numb.

So I gather their light, each shining hue,
A treasure of dreams, both ancient and new.
With a sigh of wonder, I hold them tight,
In my pocket of stars, I find my light.

Chronicles of Endless Night

In the shadows deep, a tale begins,
A chronicle born where the silence spins.
Voices of night wrap around my soul,
Each echo a memory, a life to extol.

Stars twinkle softly, secrets they keep,
While the moon casts its gaze, a vigil to sweep.
Fables and fantasies drift through the mist,
In the heart of the darkness, I'm gently kissed.

Time stretches like waves, an infinite sea,
Where every lost moment whispers to me.
Beneath the vast sky, I wander and roam,
Finding solace in the night that feels like home.

Shadows parade, a dance of their own,
In the quiet embrace, I'm never alone.
Each verse is a heartbeat, a breath in the air,
Chronicles written with love and with care.

As dawn approaches, the story unfolds,
Of courage and warmth, and the dreams that it holds.
Through endless night, I find my way bright,
With the chronicles whispered, I step into light.

Infinite Musings

Thoughts like rivers flow,
Ebbing, flowing, onward go.
Where do they lead the mind?
In silence, answers unwind.

In dreams, we find our flight,
Chasing shadows, seeking light.
Questions linger in the air,
Whispers soft, a gentle prayer.

Moments freeze in time's embrace,
Each a note in life's vast space.
In the stillness, truth reveals,
Infinite the heart's appeals.

Wander through the inner maze,
Lost in thought's hypnotic gaze.
Every turn, a brand new phase,
Life's enigma, endless ways.

As we ponder, stars ignite,
Guiding paths through darkest night.
In this dance, we seek to see,
Infinite musings, setting free.

The Silence Between Stars

In the void, a whisper sighs,
Echoing through lunar skies.
Stars in silence, softly gleam,
Woven in a cosmic dream.

Hearts beat in the quiet dark,
Tracing lines where once was spark.
Time stands still, a breath in night,
Infinite wonders, pure delight.

Galaxies in slumber stay,
Waiting for the dawning day.
In the hush of space so vast,
Moments linger, shadows cast.

Yet beneath that tranquil scene,
Lies a dance, both bright and keen.
Fleeting thoughts on starlit waves,
In the quiet, the heart braves.

Infinite realms where dreams collide,
In silence, stars become our guide.
Between the void and light, we find,
A canvas pure, where soul's aligned.

Glimpses of Distant Realms

Through the veil of time and space,
Whispers of another place.
Visions flicker, colors bright,
Dancing patterns in the night.

Across the sea of endless skies,
Hidden truths and long-lost ties.
Glimmers of a world unknown,
Where seeds of dreams are gently sown.

In the echoes, tales unfold,
Stories waiting to be told.
Ancient wishes, soft and clear,
Guide us through what we hold dear.

Each glimpse, a brush of fate,
Illuminating paths we create.
In the shadows, light persists,
Carving out what still exists.

To distant realms our spirits soar,
Searching for what lies in store.
In these glimpses, we are found,
Connected to the sacred ground.

Cosmic Whirlwinds

In the dance of planets bright,
Spirals spin through endless night.
Galactic winds, a swirling trance,
Whisper secrets, lead the dance.

Stars collide in fiery grace,
Painting colors in deep space.
Around the cosmos, forces twine,
In chaos, beauty's spark we find.

Time unwinds in vast array,
Moments caught in cosmic sway.
Each heartbeat drummed in astral song,
Guides us where we all belong.

Nature's pulse, a rhythmic flow,
Echoes through the starlit glow.
In the whirlwinds, we take flight,
Journeying through realms of light.

With every twist, a chance to dream,
Cosmic journeys, truth's bright beam.
In these whirlwinds, spirit flies,
Boundless wonder in the skies.

Celestial Whispers

In the quiet of night, dreams take flight,
Stars twinkle softly, a delicate light.
Whispers of the cosmos in sweet refrain,
Guiding lost souls through the celestial plane.

Galaxies spinning in a dance divine,
Echoes of wisdom in every line.
The moon sings softly, a lullaby bright,
Cradling the world in its silvery light.

Winds carry secrets from faraway lands,
Mapping the heavens with invisible hands.
Constellations beckon, tales to unfold,
Stories of wonder in stardust told.

A tapestry woven of silence and sound,
Infinite beauty in darkness is found.
With every heartbeat, the universe sighs,
A serenade soft beneath velvet skies.

Starlit Echoes

Beneath a shroud of ethereal glow,
Whispers of starlight begin to flow.
Each twinkling beacon, a story of old,
An echo of magic waiting to unfold.

Diadems of radiance, crowns of the night,
Embrace the horizon with shimmering light.
Dancing on air, dreams take their chance,
In the embrace of a cosmic dance.

Voices of ancients in silence reside,
Guiding the hearts that in starlight abide.
With every pulse, the heavens align,
Drawing us closer, our souls intertwine.

The night wraps us gently, a comforting cloak,
Each breath a promise, each heartbeat a note.
In these starlit echoes, we find our way,
Lost yet found in the vast Milky Way.

Cosmic Tapestry

In the loom of the night, threads intertwine,
Crafting a story through space and time.
Colors of nebulae, vibrant and bold,
Weaving our fate with the stardust of old.

Wisps of light travel from places unknown,
Brushing our spirits, we're never alone.
The fabric of dreams is stitched with care,
Each pattern a promise of love in the air.

Sailing on suns, our hopes take flight,
In galaxies far, we find our light.
With every touch, the cosmos ignites,
A canvas of wonders, enchanting nights.

Painted horizons, where stars softly weep,
Secrets of ages in silence they keep.
In the cosmic tapestry, we play our part,
Threads woven tightly, one beating heart.

Echoes of Infinity

In the vastness of space, silence speaks loud,
Echoes of infinity shrouded in cloud.
Each heartbeat a rhythm, a timeless refrain,
Singing the stories of moments that remain.

Time stretches onward, a ribbon in flight,
Moments colliding in the depth of night.
Galactic murmurs whisper secrets profound,
In the embrace of darkness, peace can be found.

Wandering stardust, we dance and we spin,
Carrying echoes of what lies within.
Embracing the journey, the unknown we seek,
In the realms of forever, we dare to speak.

Wrapped in the cosmos, we explore the divine,
Fleeting yet timeless, our souls intertwine.
Echoes of infinity, a bridge to the past,
In the circle of starlight, our shadows are cast.

Moments in the Heavens

Stars twinkle bright, in the night sky,
Whispers of dreams, drifting on high.
Moments of peace, in the vast unknown,
Hearts intertwined, never alone.

Galaxies dance, in celestial light,
Each distant world, out of our sight.
In silence we gaze, at the cosmic sea,
Wondering what could, or could not be.

Full moons glow soft, casting their spell,
Stories of old, they silently tell.
Through timeless winds, a soft embrace,
Finding our place, in the endless space.

Awakened by Nebulas

Colors collide, in a cosmic brush,
Filling the void, with a radiant rush.
Nebulas sing, of beginnings anew,
Awakening dreams, both old and true.

Mists of creation, swirling around,
Life's gentle pulse, in the mystical sound.
Whispers of stardust, cradled in air,
Painting the night, with colors rare.

Awaken the heart, to the cosmic tune,
Dance with the stars, beneath the moon.
In the embrace, of the swirling light,
Feel the magic, of endless night.

Beyond the Spiral Arms

Wander we must, past the spiral arms,
Through the cosmic weave, with its myriad charms.
Lost in the journey, yet found in the stars,
Dreamers we are, with our hopes and scars.

Beyond the horizon, where visions collide,
Finding our strength, in the universe wide.
Galactic secrets, waiting to share,
In the vastness of space, there's magic in air.

Every step forward, a heartbeat away,
Galaxies beckon, in their own play.
Beyond the known, we shall always roam,
In the cradle of night, we find our home.

Echoing Through the Firmament

Songs of the ancients, echo and flow,
Through the firmament, light years ago.
Each note a spark, in the cosmic sea,
Resonating deep, with the soul's decree.

Constellations beckon, tales to unfold,
Stars tell of journeys, both new and old.
In the shadow of night, wisdom takes flight,
Echoing softly, in the stillness of night.

Whispers of time, in the celestial dance,
Each twinkling star, a beautiful chance.
To connect with the past, and dream of the dawn,
Echoing through ages, forever drawn.

The Symphony of Distant Galaxies

Stars whisper tales of old,
In the darkness, stories unfold.
A melody from afar is heard,
In silence, the cosmos stirred.

Nebulas breathe colors bright,
Painting the vast canvas of night.
Each flicker, a note in the air,
A symphony rich, beyond compare.

Time dances in endless grace,
As light travels through endless space.
The harmony continues to flow,
In realms where only dreams can go.

Planets spin in rhythmic embrace,
Traveling paths, a celestial race.
Echoes of light, faint and sweet,
In the universe's pulse, we meet.

Together we stand, eyes alight,
Awash in the beauty of night.
For in this grandeur, we're not alone,
In the symphony, we've found our home.

A Dance of Celestial Orbits

In shadows where planets glide,
Waltzing through the cosmic tide.
Gravity's pull, a gentle sway,
Guides the dance of night and day.

Comets pirouette, tails aglow,
In ballet across the dark they flow.
Each turn a whisper, a fleeting chance,
In the grand, eternal cosmic dance.

Moons cradle worlds in soft embrace,
Circling slowly in boundless space.
Their orbits speak of time and fate,
A tapestry none can negate.

Stars join in with radiant light,
Illuminating the velvet night.
Together they spin, wild and free,
In the universe's jubilee.

As the cosmos rhythmically turns,
Fires of creation blaze and churn.
In this dance, we find our part,
Connected by the beats of the heart.

Radiant Dust and Memory

In the void, where stardust lays,
Memories linger in silent praise.
Each grain a story waiting to bloom,
From ancient chaos, they find room.

Galaxies spun from dreams and sighs,
Whispers of comets and sparkling ties.
Through the ages, they drift and spin,
Reflecting the journeys we all begin.

Time weaves a tapestry divine,
With threads of wonder and love entwined.
Moments preserved in radiant dust,
In the vastness, they gently must.

Fragments of life, both lost and found,
In cosmic echoes, a haunting sound.
As we sift through the stellar glow,
The essence of all we ever know.

In the heart of the universe's grace,
We trace the patterns time can't erase.
For in these particles, we reside,
In radiant dust, our memories abide.

The Infinite Canvas of Being

Brush strokes of light paint the sky,
Colors that dance and multiply.
Infinity stretches, vast and wide,
In this canvas, we dream and glide.

Each life a hue, vibrant and bright,
Interwoven with strands of light.
Together we craft a masterpiece,
From chaos, we find our sweet release.

Moments captured in gentle strokes,
Echoes of laughter, whispers, and hopes.
In every shadow, a story's spun,
In every heartbeat, worlds begun.

Time drips like paint, slow and sweet,
Every second, an artistic feat.
In this gallery, souls intertwine,
Creating a legacy, divine design.

As colors blend and futures call,
We find our place within it all.
For on this canvas, we truly see,
The infinite beauty of being free.

Star-Kissed Memories

In quiet nights beneath the glow,
We walk where softest breezes blow.
With every glance, a story told,
In starlit dreams, our hearts unfold.

Moments dance like fireflies bright,
Whispering secrets in the night.
We gather wishes, hopes in hand,
In star-kissed realms, together stand.

Time drifts gently, rivers flow,
Carrying tales of long ago.
Each flicker lights a cherished scene,
A tapestry of what has been.

With laughter lost in twilight's glow,
We trace the paths where memories flow.
The universe joins in our praise,
Celebrating love in endless ways.

So let us wander, hand in hand,
Through constellations, vast and grand.
For every star holds a sweet refrain,
In star-kissed memories, love remains.

Threads of Time

In the loom of life, we weave our dreams,
With every moment, stitching seams.
Threads of joy, and sorrow too,
Intertwined, in shades of blue.

Time moves softly, like a stream,
Washing over, memories gleam.
We gather remnants, hold them tight,
Creating patterns in the night.

Each whisper echoes, tales unwind,
In every corner, treasures find.
The fabric holds the stories wide,
Of love and loss, our hearts abide.

Through every season, we shall tread,
On threads of gold, where dreams are spread.
With gentle hands, we'll weave anew,
Crafting life with colors true.

So let us cherish, every thread,
In this tapestry, softly spread.
For time, though fleeting, leaves a mark,
In threads of time, our souls embark.

Hued Horizons

At dawn, the sky ignites in flame,
A canvas vast, we call its name.
With every hue, the world awakes,
In splendor grand, the silence breaks.

Soft pastels blend with golden rays,
Nature's palette in bright displays.
Whispers of morning, soft and sweet,
Awake the dreams in every heartbeat.

As noon arrives, the colors shift,
Bold and vibrant, nature's gift.
Through shades of green, and azure skies,
Beauty dances before our eyes.

As dusk approaches, shadows grow,
The horizon glows with a warm glow.
Crimson and violet bleed and fade,
A gentle sigh, the day displayed.

In twilight's embrace, we find our peace,
Hued horizons whisper, sweet release.
With every sunset, a promise made,
That beauty lingers, never strayed.

Flickers in the Night Sky

Under the vast, a velvet sea,
Stars like diamonds, wild and free.
They sparkle softly, winking bright,
Flickers of magic in the night.

As moonbeams laugh on silver streams,
We chase the echoes of our dreams.
The constellations, stories unfold,
Silent whispers of the bold.

With every twinkle, wishes soar,
Carried on wings, they start to explore.
In darkness, hope finds a spark,
Flickers of light, igniting the dark.

In the quiet, secrets shared,
With every star, a heart laid bare.
We gather moments, scattered bright,
In flickers, we find pure delight.

So look above, with eyes so wide,
Embrace the night, let dreams collide.
For in the flickers, life will show,
The beauty of moments, set aglow.

Celestial Whispers

In the quiet night sky, stars gleam,
Whispering secrets in silver beams.
Gentle breezes stir the dark,
Echoes of dreams, a luminous spark.

Moonlight dances on the waves,
Caressing hearts, the night behaves.
Softly calling through the night,
Guiding souls with its pure light.

Constellations weave stories old,
Tales of love, adventure bold.
Galaxies swirl, a cosmic song,
In their embrace, we all belong.

Voices from the depths of space,
In every heartbeat, we find grace.
Stars align, a celestial tune,
Binding our hopes 'neath the same moon.

Time drifts softly, a fragile thread,
Connecting dreams to where we tread.
With each whisper, the night unfolds,
Endless wonders in tales retold.

Starlit Echoes

In the stillness, starlight glows,
Whispers drift on gentle flows.
Echoes of laughter linger near,
In the cosmos, love's sincere.

Fleeting moments slip away,
Captured in the twilight's play.
Every heartbeat, an echo sings,
Valleys wide, on moonlit wings.

Atlas of dreams spreads wide and far,
Guided by the evening star.
Hopes entwined in cosmic dust,
In starlit skies, we place our trust.

Rippling galaxies hum a tune,
Crafting dreams 'neath the pale moon.
Light-years sing of paths we roam,
In every whisper, we find home.

The night expands with every sigh,
Beneath the veil of the midnight sky.
In the hush, our hearts unite,
As starlit echoes fill the night.

Infinity's Shattered Reflections

In the mirrored depths of time,
Shattered whispers, a silent chime.
Fragments of dreams, lost in space,
Infinity's grasp, our haunted trace.

Each moment dances, a fleeting spark,
Echoing voices in the dark.
Reflections of what could have been,
In every shadow, shadows within.

Waves of longing crash and flow,
Carving paths where memories grow.
A tapestry rich, yet bittersweet,
In every heartbeat, life's heartbeat.

Through fog and stars our journeys blend,
Finding solace in the bends.
Each reflection, a story to tell,
In shattered pieces, we find ourselves.

Time stretches like a silver thread,
Interwoven with dreams unsaid.
In infinity's dance, we seek release,
Among shattered reflections, find peace.

Cosmic Tapestries Unraveled

Threads of starlight weave the night,
Cosmic tales in clusters bright.
Woven whispers, each color bold,
In the tapestry, stories unfold.

Galaxies twinkle, their secrets shared,
With every heartbeat, a moment spared.
As the universe spins and sways,
Dancing threads in celestial ways.

Nebulas bloom with colors rare,
Painting the void with vibrant flair.
In the fabric of time, dreams entwined,
Infinite wonders, intertwined.

Echoes of stars follow the breeze,
Filling the night with mysteries.
In every corner, a tale ajar,
Woven dreams beneath the stars.

As the cosmos hums its ancient tune,
We find our place in the silver moon.
In cosmic tapestries, we're all part,
Threads of existence, a unified heart.

Cosmic Collage

In the canvas of night, stars align,
Colors twirl and dance, so divine,
Galaxies whisper secrets untold,
In the vast expanse, dreams unfold.

Nebulas bloom, a painter's delight,
Shadows of comets, streaks of light,
Planets waltz in a cosmic embrace,
Eclipses hide, then reveal their grace.

The universe hums a melodic tune,
Time drifts softly like a silver moon,
Stardust sprinkled on twilight's brew,
Awakening wonders, forever new.

Each constellation maps a heart's beat,
Journeys woven with fate's soft thread,
Voices of ancients echo on high,
In this collage beneath the sky.

So gather your dreams, let them take flight,
Join the dance of the endless night,
In the cosmic love that we all share,
We are stardust, floating in the air.

Orbits of Time

Circles spun 'round the sun's embrace,
Time lingers on, a gentle trace,
Hours shimmer like diamonds in flight,
Weaving through day and dipping to night.

Epochs collide in a rhythmic sway,
Moments cascade like waves in the bay,
Past and future, a delicate blend,
In the dance of time, all things mend.

A clock's whisper echoes in space,
Chimes of eternity, a warm embrace,
Every second, a pearl on a string,
Infinite treasures the hours bring.

In cycles that move, we find our place,
Each heartbeat aligned with the cosmic race,
Footprints we leave in the sands of the past,
Orbits of time spinning ever vast.

So pause for a breath, and let it be,
In the galaxies, we are all free,
For in this grand clockwork, we are the rhyme,
Forever united in orbits of time.

Celestial Chains

Bound by the pulls of the unseen threads,
Galactic links where the wanderer treads,
Comets and planets, they dance and sway,
In chains of light, they find their way.

Gravity whispers, a lover's call,
Binding the fates of the great and small,
Nebulas cradle the lost and found,
In this cosmic web, we're tightly wound.

From supernova's birth to black hole's clasp,
Every echo of light is a fleeting gasp,
Stars twinkle softly, a sign of our kin,
In celestial chains, we all begin.

Together we journey through night's soft glow,
Riding the rays that the ancients know,
Climbing the heights of the ether's expanse,
In the universal song, we join the dance.

So look to the heavens, let your heart sing,
In chains of the cosmos, we are the spring,
A tapestry woven from starlight's thread,
Celestial chains binding us ahead.

Celestial Journeys

Eons of travels through the astral sea,
Comets blaze trails where the courage be,
Constellations guide us through shadow and light,
On celestial journeys, hearts take flight.

With every tick of the cosmic clock,
We sail through the heavens, an eternal walk,
Stardust trails mark the paths of old,
Stories of wanderers waiting to be told.

Across the vastness, horizons blend,
With dreams in our sails, on starlit winds we depend,
Each planet a chapter, each star a friend,
In this boundless realm, the journeys extend.

Galaxies swirl like dancers in trance,
Filling the sky with a cosmic romance,
Travelers roam where the sun meets the moon,
In the light of the dawn, we find our tune.

So gather your will, let your spirit soar,
In celestial journeys, we're forever more,
Through the tapestry woven, we find our grace,
As we wander the cosmos, a boundless space.

Cosmic Lullabies

Stars whisper softly in night's sweet embrace,
Dreams take flight in the vastness of space.
Galaxies twinkle, a soft lull made,
Rest your eyes, in their glow you'll wade.

Nebulae cradle the hopes we hold tight,
Cradled by darkness, the universe bright.
Moonbeams gently kiss the earth below,
Guiding our hearts where starlight will flow.

Planets spin slowly, in rhythm they move,
Each cosmic rhythm, a lullaby's groove.
Time drifts like stardust, sparkling and free,
In cosmic harmonies, we find our glee.

Infinite wonders, they sing through the night,
With every heartbeat, our spirits take flight.
In the silence of space, our dreams intertwine,
Cosmic lullabies, forever divine.

Here in the heavens, our worries release,
Floating on starlight, we find our peace.
In the arms of the universe, we lay,
Swayed by the whispers of night and day.

The Dance of Light

In the stillness of dusk, shadows take flight,
The world twirls softly, kissed by the light.
Colors collide in a vibrant parade,
Nature's own canvas, where dreams are displayed.

Flickers of gold paint the edges of trees,
Waltzing with breezes, they sway with such ease.
A symphony plays as the daylight fades,
Whispers of twilight in balmy cascades.

Stars take their cue, twinkling with grace,
Each one a partner in this endless trace.
Celestial bodies in perfect array,
Dancing together in the night's ballet.

Moonlight reflects on the rippling stream,
Creating a vision, a radiant dream.
Echoes of laughter bring warmth to the night,
All are united in this dance of light.

So let us all join in this cosmic waltz,
Where every heartbeat with joyousness exalts.
In the ballroom of stars, our spirits take flight,
Forever enchanted by the dance of light.

Celestial Portals

Through the veil of night, a doorway appears,
Leading to realms beyond laughter and tears.
Stardust collected, like dreams in a jar,
Wonders await us, both near and afar.

Motionless silence, a passage unfolds,
Stories of universe, silently told.
Galaxies beckon us, bright as a spark,
Guiding our journey through the shadow's dark.

In the heart of a comet, a secret so pure,
Wisdom of ages in paths we assure.
Each star a beacon, shining so bright,
Illuminating corners with celestial light.

Boundless horizons, where time does unwind,
Every glance forward, new treasures to find.
In every portal, a tale to embrace,
Carved in the fabric of infinite space.

So step through the gateways, let spirit take flight,
The cosmos is waiting, alive with delight.
With each breath we take, let wonders commence,
In celestial realms, we'll find our essence.

Melodies of the Milky Way

Whispers of music in the starry expanse,
Notes weave together in a cosmic dance.
Planets align to the rhythm of night,
Melodies echo, soft and bright.

Galaxies hum in sweet harmony,
Choruses carried by the cosmic sea.
Sailing through starlight, our hearts take part,
In the symphony played from the universe's heart.

Nebulae vibrate with colors so deep,
Gentle reminders that freedom we keep.
Each twinkle a note, each shimmer a song,
In the vastness of space, we all belong.

As orbs of light twirl in a grand ballet,
The music of cosmos guides our way.
Together we sing, beneath the night's sway,
Lost in the magic of Milky Way's play.

So let the notes fill up the night air,
As we dance with the stars without a care.
For in this moment, in cosmic display,
Life becomes music in the Milky Way.

Echoing Hearts

In whispers soft, the night does call,
Two souls entwined, they rise and fall.
Beneath the stars, their secrets flow,
Echoes linger, where love might grow.

The moonlight dances on their skin,
In every sigh, a world within.
With every pulse, the moments blend,
A timeless song, where hearts transcend.

Through shadows deep, they wander far,
Guided by dreams, like distant stars.
In whispers shared, their fates unite,
As echoes fade into the night.

With hands entwined, they brave the storm,
Together, hearts both fierce and warm.
In gentle tides, they find their way,
As echoes whisper, come what may.

Their laughter rings through twilight's hue,
A melody of love so true.
In every heartbeat, they reside,
Echoing love, forever tied.

Light Beneath the Surface

In still waters, shadows play,
Where secrets rest, and feelings stray.
A glimmer shines, a subtle ray,
Beneath the calm, the dreams delay.

Ripples form with every thought,
In depths unseen, all battles fought.
A dance of light, both faint and clear,
As echoes rise, the heart draws near.

Expectations float on fleeting tides,
With every wave, the truth abides.
A journey deep, where courage swells,
In silent realms, the spirit dwells.

A lantern's glow on shores unknown,
In whispered winds, hope is sown.
Through trials faced, the heart finds peace,
As light emerges, doubts release.

Connection's spark beneath the deep,
Awakens dreams that softly seep.
In every heart, a beacon bright,
A promise held beyond the night.

Timeless Wanderings

Across the fields where time stands still,
Two spirits dance, with hearts to fill.
Through ages past, they find their song,
In whispered winds, where they belong.

The sun sets low, in golden hues,
As shadows stretch, they chase the blues.
With open hearts, they roam the lands,
In every step, fate's gentle hands.

Mountains rise, and oceans vast,
In every journey, memories cast.
Together they weave, through light and dark,
A tapestry rich, a sacred mark.

Seasons change, but love remains,
Through stormy nights and sunny gains.
In laughter shared, and tears they find,
Timeless bonds, forever kind.

With every sunrise, they embrace,
The fleeting joys that life will grace.
In wanderlust, their spirits roar,
Through timeless paths, forever more.

Mysteries of the Celestial Sea

Beneath the stars, where secrets hide,
The cosmos spins, a timeless tide.
With cosmic waves, the heart must sail,
In mysteries deep, where dreams prevail.

Galaxies swirl in vibrant hue,
A dance of fate, both old and new.
In every twinkle, stories told,
Of love eternal, worth more than gold.

The moon a guide, through shadowed night,
Illuminating paths with silver light.
In whispered prayers, the stardust calls,
Together wandering through celestial walls.

With every glance at skies above,
They seek the truth, the endless love.
In cosmic realms, their spirits soar,
Mysteries beckon, forevermore.

As comets streak and meteors fall,
They find their peace within it all.
The universe sings, a lullaby sweet,
In the celestial sea, their hearts will meet.

The Flicker of Existence

In shadows cast by fleeting light,
We find our place, a spark ignites.
Moments drift like autumn leaves,
Whispers lost in evening's eves.

Each heartbeat echoes through the night,
A ghostly dance in starry flight.
Time dissolves like morning mist,
Yet every touch remains, persist.

Like fireflies that paint the dark,
Our souls entwined, a vibrant spark.
We chase the dawn, the warmth we crave,
In the flicker, we are brave.

Life's tapestry, a thread so fine,
Stitched in tales of yours and mine.
With every breath, we weave the dream,
In existence's fragile stream.

The flicker fades but never dies,
In memory's heart, the light defies.
A timeless bond that ever glows,
In gentle waves, existence flows.

Celestial Moments Suspended

Beneath the arch of endless skies,
Stars twinkle softly, ancient ties.
A moment caught, a breath held still,
In cosmic dance, we bend to will.

The moonlight spills on silent seas,
Gentle waves sing whispered pleas.
Time pauses like a painter's brush,
In fleeting beauty, hearts will hush.

Glimmers of fate in twilight's haze,
Each star a note in night's vast gaze.
Echoes linger, sweet and warm,
In celestial calm, we transform.

Tides of silver pull us near,
Moments held where dreams appear.
In soft embraces, soft like dew,
The universe speaks, just we two.

Suspended time in love's embrace,
A fleeting glance, a sacred space.
In every heartbeat, secrets blend,
In celestial moments, we transcend.

Nebulae in the Mind's Eye

In the depths of thoughts, colors swirl,
Nebulae bloom, galaxies unfurl.
Imagination paints a vibrant scene,
Where echoes dance, and whispers lean.

Stars are born in darkness deep,
While dreams awaken from their sleep.
Each thought a spark, a cosmic flare,
In the mind's eye, we dare to scare.

Visions drift like clouds of light,
Radiant hues in the quiet night.
Fleeting wonders cascade like rain,
In our mind's eye, joy, and pain.

Stardust settles on silent shores,
The universe whispers, opens doors.
In the kaleidoscope of dreams we roam,
In nebulae, we find our home.

Thoughts collide, a cosmic dance,
Where time and space merge in a glance.
Infinite realms that we explore,
In the mind's eye, forevermore.

Whispered Secrets of the Cosmos

Stars align in silent grace,
Echoes whisper through empty space.
The cosmos speaks in subtle tones,
Secrets hidden in starry stones.

Galaxies weave the tales of old,
In cosmic fires, mysteries unfold.
Each twinkle tells of journeys long,
In the void, we learn to belong.

Among the comets, tales are spun,
In every flight, a race begun.
And as we listen to the night,
Lost dreams emerge in the soft light.

The universe hums a gentle song,
In whispered secrets, where we belong.
Hidden realms waiting to be found,
In the silence, our hearts resound.

In stellar nurseries, life begins,
With every breath, a world spins.
We chase the stars, our spirits free,
In whispered secrets, just you and me.

The Essence of Time

Ticking softly through the night,
Moments whisper, taking flight.
Each second holds a tale to tell,
In time's embrace, we rise and fell.

Drifting sands in endless grace,
Mark the journey, set our pace.
Footsteps echo, memories fade,
Yet in the heart, they're never swayed.

Days turn into fleeting dreams,
Merging laughter with silent screams.
The clock unwinds, we watch in awe,
For time reveals the unspoken law.

Past and future intertwine,
In the present, we align.
Moments cherished, lost in light,
The essence of time, day and night.

So let us dance and seize the day,
In every heartbeat, find our way.
For within this fleeting chime,
We hold the essence of all time.

Horizons of Light

At dawn's first blush, the world awakes,
Colors dance, a song it makes.
Promises whispered on the breeze,
In every ray, our hearts find ease.

Golden skies embrace the night,
Guiding souls with gentle light.
Dreamers wander, hopes ignite,
Through every shadow, love's pure sight.

Stars twinkle like distant dreams,
Each one sharing what it seems.
Horizons stretch, inviting grace,
Life unfolds in this vast space.

The evening paints with hues of fire,
As dusk descends, we lift our choir.
Voices rise, breaking the dark,
In each heart, a glowing spark.

Together under skies of gold,
We chase the stories yet untold.
Horizons of light forever shine,
In every moment, yours and mine.

Cosmic Reflections

Beneath the stars, a canvas wide,
Galaxies swirl, the great divide.
Each glimmer holds a secret deep,
In cosmic whispers, dreams we keep.

Echoes of time in stardust glow,
Vast horizons where wonders flow.
Moments caught in twilight's grace,
Reflections spark, we find our place.

Planets dance in a silent waltz,
Weaving fate without a fault.
In the shadows of the night,
We discover paths of endless light.

Through the cosmos, our spirits soar,
Chasing dreams forevermore.
In every star, a chance we find,
To embrace the universe, unconfined.

Celestial whispers call us near,
Guiding us through the vast frontier.
Cosmic reflections shining bright,
In the depths of endless night.

From Stardust to Dreams

Born from stardust, we arise,
Carried forth on whispered sighs.
In the midnight's tender gleam,
We chase the echoes of a dream.

Each moment stitched with silver thread,
Weaving futures in colors spread.
Hearts ignited by cosmic fire,
From such depths, our souls aspire.

Floating gently on the breeze,
Finding solace in the trees.
The moonlight guides our every quest,
In dreams, our wishful hearts find rest.

Journey on through endless night,
Chasing shadows, seeking light.
From stardust, we shall rise anew,
Crafting dreams in radiant hue.

Together we weave the tapestry,
Of hopes and dreams, a symphony.
From stardust to dreams, we fly,
With each breath, we touch the sky.

Celestial Surfaces

The moonlight dances on the sea,
Whispers of stars in harmony.
Galaxies spin in silent grace,
Painting dreams in endless space.

A comet trails a fleeting spark,
Illuminating shadows dark.
Constellations tell their tales,
In every breath, the cosmos hails.

Through velvet skies where silence sighs,
The universe in joyful cries.
Each twinkle holds a wish so bright,
Guiding hearts through cosmic night.

Time drifts softly, stars align,
Moments crafted, pure divine.
In every wink, fate's design,
Echos of the grand design.

Hearts of stardust, dreams unfold,
In the vastness, stories told.
Celestial surfaces, realms anew,
In every glance, wonder's hue.

Visions of the Nebula

A swirl of colors in cosmic mist,
Echoes of love that coexist.
Wonders hidden in each cloud,
In silent beauty, I'm allowed.

Nebulae dream in soft embrace,
Carving stories in endless space.
Whispers of time, forever told,
In every hue, a spark of gold.

Fragments dance, a radiant show,
Galactic rivers ebb and flow.
Visions born from starlit night,
Awakening the heart's delight.

In cosmic art, our hopes entwine,
A map of dreams where spirits shine.
Every shimmer, a wish bestowed,
In nebula's heart, dreams are sowed.

From crimson to blue, the colors sing,
Each a truth that stars will bring.
Visions of the nebula, bright and free,
In the dance of eternity.

Galactic Echoes

In silence vast, the echoes call,
A haunting song that binds us all.
Galaxies hum their ancient tune,
Underneath the watchful moon.

Starfields shimmer, a wondrous glow,
Stories woven in twilight's flow.
Fragments of light from long ago,
Galactic whispers, soft and slow.

Every pulse, a memory flows,
In the void where stillness grows.
Echoes of wonders we have known,
In every heart, the seeds are sown.

A journey through the cosmic night,
Searching for the truth and light.
Galactic echoes guide our way,
In a canvas where dreams play.

Stars fade gently, the night drifts on,
But in our minds, the songs are strong.
Galactic echoes ever near,
In the universe, we persevere.

Starlit Soliloquies

In the hush of night, stars convene,
Whispers of fate in silent sheen.
Each flicker a thought, a story shared,
In starlit soliloquies, we're bared.

Midnight dreams take form and rise,
Beneath the gaze of endless skies.
Voices of ancients, soft and wise,
Guide the heart where the cosmos lies.

Through the vastness, secrets flow,
In shimmering waves, love will grow.
Every twinkle, a promise kept,
In the silence, the universe wept.

In this expanse, we find our place,
In moonlit shadows, we embrace.
Starlit dreams weave time's array,
In every heartbeat, night and day.

So let us dance amongst the stars,
Join the melodies that are ours.
Starlit soliloquies we sing,
In each moment, the cosmos spring.

Beyond the Known

In shadows deep, where whispers dwell,
A path unfolds, the silent swell.
Through misty veils, the secrets roam,
Beyond the known, we seek our home.

The stars above, they guide our way,
In twilight's grasp, we start to play.
Each step we take, a dance with fate,
Beyond the known, we find our state.

With open hearts, we chase the light,
Through cosmic dreams that pierce the night.
In realms unknown, our spirits soar,
Beyond the known, forevermore.

Each heartbeat sings of endless dreams,
In tapestry of silver seams.
We wander far, yet never stray,
Beyond the known, we make our play.

So let us leap, let's break the chains,
Embrace the wild, release our reins.
With every breath, a chance we take,
Beyond the known, our souls awake.

Stellar Reveries

In tranquil nights, where silence reigns,
Stellar reveries break earthly chains.
With twinkling lights, our dreams take flight,
In cosmic waves, we merge with night.

Comets pass with tales untold,
In frozen paths of shimmering gold.
Each spark ignites the heart's desire,
Stellar reveries, our souls conspire.

Amid the dark, a glow appears,
A gentle balm for mortal fears.
With every glance, our spirits rise,
Stellar reveries, beyond the skies.

In whispers soft, the stars converse,
In endless love, we break the curse.
Through stardust dreams, we find our way,
Stellar reveries, come what may.

So close your eyes, let visions greet,
In shimmering paths, our souls will meet.
With every heartbeat, let us sway,
Stellar reveries, forever play.

Unraveled Threads of Existence

In the fabric of time, we weave,
With strands that shimmer, then leave.
Each knot tells stories of yore,
Frayed edges whisper, forevermore.

Fates collide in the twilight hue,
Echoing dreams that once felt true.
Paths diverge in a dance so grand,
Hands reaching out, yet apart we stand.

Moments linger, fragile and frail,
Bound by whispers of love's soft trail.
The cosmos spins in a timeless ballet,
Every heartbeat sings what words can't say.

Lost in the maze of our own design,
We seek the light, the stars align.
A tapestry woven of hope and despair,
In the quiet spaces, we find solace there.

Threads of existence, tangled, entwined,
A journey of hearts, forever aligned.
In the unraveling, we discover the truth,
Life's greatest lesson resides in our youth.

Echoing Stars and Light's Lament

Stars whisper secrets across the night,
Echoing dreams, weaving delight.
In the silence, their brilliance gleams,
Filling the void with forgotten dreams.

Each shimmer tells tales of the past,
A glimpse of futures that fade so fast.
Light's lament, a soft sigh in the air,
Echoing wisdom, whispered with care.

Galaxies spiral in celestial dance,
Inviting the lost to take a chance.
Through the darkness, their glow remains,
Carrying echoes of love's sweet strains.

In the stillness, we hear their plight,
Guiding lost souls through the night.
They beckon us forth, to touch and to feel,
In each heartbeat, a promise to heal.

The cosmos calls with a gentle embrace,
Holding our dreams in its infinite grace.
As we journey on, hand in hand,
Lost in the music of a starlit band.

The Silent Song of Astral Fields

Across the sky, where silence dwells,
Astral fields weave their magic spells.
The quiet hum of infinite space,
Conducts a symphony, a timeless grace.

In shadows deep, the stars awake,
Singing softly, no steps to take.
Each twinkle carries a silent plea,
To listen close, to set our hearts free.

Galactic whispers, secrets of light,
Dance in the dark, a wondrous sight.
With every breath, we feel the beat,
Of the universe's rhythmic heartbeat.

Through endless nights, we roam and dream,
In the cosmos' vast and tender seam.
A silent song, a lullaby sweet,
Cradles our souls at the starlit street.

As we wander through this cosmic sea,
We find our place, we learn to be.
In the silent song, we'll always remain,
Connected, alive, in joy and in pain.

Shadows of Luminary Realms

In twilight's embrace, shadows reside,
Guardians of secrets, where dreams abide.
Luminary realms, both near and far,
Guide the lost souls beneath each star.

Whispers of wisdom, carried on air,
Awaken our hearts to the beauty laid bare.
In the stillness, we find our way,
As shadows of light dance and sway.

Each flicker of hope, a flame in the night,
Illuminates paths, wrongs made right.
Chasing the shadows, we learn to see,
The depth of existence, the essence of free.

With every heartbeat, a promise unfolds,
Echoes of stories, yet to be told.
In luminary realms, our spirits unite,
Navigating through darkness, toward the light.

Together we rise, as shadows take flight,
In the dance of existence, igniting the night.
A tapestry woven of stars and dreams,
In shadows of realms, our true light beams.

Cosmic Kaleidoscope

Swirling colors drift in space,
Mirrors reflect a starry face,
Galaxies dance in silent tune,
Wonders bloom beneath the moon.

Fragments of light gently collide,
In this vast realm where dreams abide,
Stardust whispers in cosmic play,
Eternal night, then breaks to day.

Nebulas burst with vibrant hues,
Creating patterns, old yet new,
Each spark a tale of time and fate,
Weaving stories that resonate.

In every twist, a secret lies,
A universe behind our eyes,
As worlds collide, we find our place,
In the grand dance of boundless space.

Through every shift and every turn,
A lesson learned, a truth to earn,
Cosmic wonders echo near,
In this kaleidoscope of fear.

Illuminated Paradoxes

Shadows cast in glowing light,
Truth and fiction intertwine,
Paths we walk, both dark and bright,
In the puzzle, we define.

Every tear a silver thread,
Woven in a tapestry,
The things we lose, the things we dread,
Shape our shared tapestry.

Silent echoes of the past,
Speak of battles left undone,
Moments linger, shadows cast,
In the dance of moon and sun.

In contradictions, we discern,
Lessons learned in twisted fate,
For every candle's flame, we yearn,
Illuminated paths await.

Embrace the chaos, hold it tight,
For in the dark, we find the spark,
Paradoxes shining bright,
Guide us through the endless dark.

Celestial Fractals

Patterns unfold through time and space,
Infinite loops, a mystic trace,
Each spiral whispers timeless lore,
In fractal dreams, we search for more.

Stars align in sacred dance,
Chaos births a hidden chance,
Cosmic echoes, voices blend,
In fractals where beginnings end.

Nature's art, a grand design,
Mountains rise, and rivers twine,
Every leaf, a life reflected,
In this fractal world, connected.

As universe expands and bends,
Truths converge, and form descends,
Heartbeats echo, worlds align,
In every pattern, we divine.

Through each fragment, we see the whole,
Threads of life interlace the soul,
Fractal journeys, endless flight,
Leading us towards the light.

Dreams in the Dark Void

In the stillness, shadows creep,
Whispers linger, secrets keep,
Silent thoughts in velvet night,
Guide us through the endless fright.

Stars are dreams, flickering bright,
Casting hope in the dark fright,
In the void, possibility,
Awaits patiently to be.

Lost in silence, we embrace,
The wonder of this empty space,
Where imagination takes its flight,
Through the fabric of the night.

In every corner, silence hums,
Creating songs where darkness drums,
Dreams emerge from ghostly lines,
In the void, the spirit shines.

So let us wander, hand in hand,
Through dreams we weave and understand,
In the dark, beauty resides,
In the void, a world abides.

Whispers of the Void

In silence deep, the shadows play,
Stars murmur secrets, drift away.
Emptiness holds a haunting sound,
Where lost dreams and echoes abound.

Veils of darkness softly blend,
Where beginnings and endings wend.
A fleeting moment, time does bend,
In the vastness, we ascend.

Ghostly whispers brush my skin,
Calling forth what lies within.
Endless night wraps me tight,
Guiding hearts to find the light.

Unseen forces shape the night,
Cradled in boundless night's flight.
A waltz of shadows' gentle grace,
Whispers of the void's embrace.

In the dark, the cosmos gleams,
Weaving through our ancient dreams.
Eternal dance, we spin and sway,
Lost in time, we fade away.

Threads of the Universe

Woven starlight, fine and bright,
Connects the worlds in silent night.
Each thread a tale, a path unknown,
In the fabric of time, we've grown.

Galaxies swirl, a painter's brush,
Colors of dreams in a cosmic rush.
Bound together, our fates entwine,
In the dance of space, we align.

Shimmering strands of destiny,
Guiding us through eternity.
With every pull, a story spun,
Echoes of all, the two become one.

Each flicker of light, a whispered wish,
A cosmic bond that none can miss.
Threads of time, together we weave,
Into the tapestry we believe.

In the quiet, the cosmos sings,
Of ancient hopes and new beginnings.
In the loom of fate, we find our place,
Threads of the universe, an endless grace.

Astral Memories

Fleeting glimpses from far-off skies,
Echoes of laughter, cosmic sighs.
In the night's cradle, memories gleam,
A starlit journey, a glowing dream.

Phantoms of time in endless drift,
Whispering tales, a timeless gift.
Brushing against the veil of night,
In every memory, stars ignite.

Glimmers of love that once did bloom,
In the shadows where galaxies loom.
Every heartbeat, a thread held tight,
In astral realms, we find our light.

Through the vastness, we wander free,
Beneath the gaze of infinity.
Moments captured, soft and bright,
In astral memories, we unite.

Beyond the stars, where dreams collide,
In cosmic whispers, we confide.
With every heartbeat, we find our way,
Astral memories guide our stay.

Timeless Constellations

In the night's embrace, we find our kin,
Timeless constellations spin within.
Each star a story, ancient and bold,
Whispers of the past, softly told.

Galaxies dance in celestial light,
Guardians of dreams in endless night.
Mapmakers of fate, they call our name,
In starlit paths, we play the game.

A tapestry woven with care and grace,
Threads of light in a boundless space.
Guiding sailors on seas unknown,
Constellations, our way has grown.

In their glow, our hopes take flight,
A dance of shadows and purest light.
Timeless wonders, we gaze in awe,
As dreams unfold with each star's draw.

Connected forever, we share a fate,
In the heavens, we elevate.
Timeless constellations shine so bright,
In their embrace, we find our light.

Cosmic Perspectives

In galaxies far, wonders unfold,
Stars weave stories, mysteries told.
Nebulas dance in colors bright,
Across the canvas of the night.

Planets spin in silent grace,
Orbiting dreams in endless space.
Time unfolds like a cosmic scroll,
Whispering secrets to the soul.

Light years stretch into the vast,
Connecting futures with the past.
Each comet trails a fleeting blaze,
Guiding travelers through the haze.

In the dark, our thoughts take flight,
Braving depths of endless night.
We seek the paths the stars have traced,
In the cosmos, we embrace.

So let us roam through boundless skies,
With open hearts and curious eyes.
In the dance of time and space,
We find our place in this grand race.

Harmonies of the Spheres

The planets hum a gentle tune,
As melodies drift 'neath the moon.
Saturn's rings in whispers sway,
While Jupiter's storms hold night at bay.

Celestial bodies, a vast ballet,
Moving in patterns, a cosmic display.
Each note a breath in the void unheard,
Creating a symphony, softly stirred.

With every orbit, they align,
A harmony divine and fine.
Galaxies spiral in rapt delight,
Echoing secrets of the night.

Waves of starlight travel near,
Transcending all we hold dear.
In every sound, a story to tell,
Of life's embrace, weaves its spell.

So listen close to the night sky's song,
A serenade that's vast and strong.
In the cosmos, we find our part,
A fusion of science and art.

Beliefs of the Infinite

In whispers soft, the universe calls,
Echoing dreams down cosmic halls.
Faith in realms we cannot see,
Beliefs of ancient mystery.

Stars align with purpose clear,
Guiding souls through doubt and fear.
In every heart, a flicker's spark,
A quest for meaning in the dark.

The void can cradle dreams anew,
As hopes take flight on stardust dew.
In every grain of cosmic sand,
Lies the touch of a guiding hand.

Weaving tales in the great unseen,
Between the lines of what has been.
Our spirits dance in endless flight,
Chasing echoes of pure light.

In infinity, we find our way,
Through shadows deep, to break of day.
With every breath, we seek, we strive,
In endless love, we come alive.

In the Arms of Light

In the dawn's embrace, shadows wane,
Illuminated paths call again.
Gentle beams paint the morning sky,
While dreams awaken and take to fly.

Golden rays kiss the earth, so sweet,
Unfolding magic beneath our feet.
In the arms of light, we find our grace,
A soft caress, a warm embrace.

Through every moment, brilliance flows,
Guiding us where love yet grows.
The universe hums a radiant song,
In its arms, we all belong.

With every sunset, colors blend,
A symphony of light, transcending end.
In twilight's glow, the stars ignite,
Holding us close in the fabric of night.

Connected in love's brilliant beam,
We journey together, dream by dream.
For in the light, we take our stand,
Creating future hand in hand.

Echoes of the Celestial Sea

Whispers dance in the cosmic breeze,
Stars compose melodies with ease.
Galaxies spin, a celestial swirl,
Echoes of light in the night unfurl.

Waves of stardust, soft and bright,
Illuminate the depths of the night.
Planets hum in a tranquil tune,
Cradled gently by the silver moon.

Infinite depths where dreams reside,
In the dark water, we must abide.
Sailing through realms of unseen grace,
We drift on waves in this timeless space.

Reflections shimmer, a cosmic sea,
Endless wonders await you and me.
With each heartbeat, our spirits soar,
Boundless journeys forevermore.

The Veil of Time's Embrace

In the hush of dusk, secrets lie,
A tapestry woven beneath the sky.
Moments trapped in a timeless fold,
Whispers of ages in shadows bold.

Each heartbeat echoes throughout the years,
Faint silhouettes of laughter and tears.
Time's gentle touch, a lover's hand,
Guiding us softly through this vast land.

Memories linger like petals in air,
Floating through spaces, silent and rare.
The present dances with the past's grace,
In the veil of time's tender embrace.

Step through the portal, let go of fear,
Find solace within what has brought us here.
In the heart of the now, our spirits align,
Awash in the glow of the stars that shine.

Galactic Dreams in Twilight

At twilight's edge, dreams take flight,
Galactic wonders fade into night.
Stars shimmer softly, a whispered call,
Inviting our hearts to rise and fall.

Nebulas bloom like flowers in space,
Colors blending in a slow embrace.
We journey through realms where visions gleam,
Lost in the rhythm of a cosmic dream.

The cosmos twirls in a dance divine,
As starlit pathways weave and entwine.
Floating on currents of time and space,
We chase the shadows, we run the race.

In this twilight, we find our way,
Guided by light that will never sway.
Galactic whispers fill the air,
A symphony of dreams beyond compare.

Shards of the Night Sky

Scattered diamonds on velvet blue,
Fragments of tales the cosmos knew.
Each star a story, a life once lived,
Shards of the night sky, secrets they give.

Meteor trails blaze paths so bold,
Glittering whispers of legends told.
In their glow, we find our place,
Connected through time in this vast space.

Constellations paint the canvas bright,
Guiding our dreams through the endless night.
Navigators of hope and desire,
With every twinkle, we lift higher.

The sky unfolds its celestial hand,
Inviting us all to see and stand.
In shards of wonder, we find our way,
Under the night sky where spirits play.

Lightyears of Wonder

In the sky, bright dreams appear,
Twinkling stars, so far yet near.
Galaxies whisper, secrets unfold,
Stories of starlight, wonders untold.

Nebulas dance in hues of blue,
A canvas vast, imagination true.
Planets spinning in a cosmic waltz,
Time suspends, no room for faults.

A quiet night, the universe sighs,
Echoes of ages, light never dies.
Each flicker a hope, a wish on the wing,
In lightyears of wonder, our spirits sing.

Vast horizons of shimmer and glow,
Endless journeys where dreams can flow.
In the darkness, we find our way,
Guided by stars that never sway.

So let us drift on this celestial sea,
Boundless and bright, forever free.
For in the cosmos, we're never apart,
Lightyears of wonder dwell in our heart.

Cosmic Sketches

With a brush of light, I paint the sky,
Each star a dot where dreams can fly.
Galactic swirls, in colors grand,
A cosmic canvas, a universe planned.

Comets streak like thoughts unchained,
Chasing time, joy uncontained.
Meteors whisper tales of old,
In cosmic sketches, our fates unfold.

Nebulae bloom like flowers rare,
In the void, a painter's care.
Strokes of brilliance, shadows entwined,
In every corner, new truths to find.

Eclipses tease with light and dark,
Echoes of ages leaving their mark.
Constellations dance, a timeless show,
In the night, dreams gently flow.

So take my hand, let's wander wide,
In cosmic sketches, let love be our guide.
With stardust and wonder, we'll leave our trace,
In the gallery of time, an endless space.

Patterns of the Infinite

In the spiral arms of galaxies,
There lies a map of destinies.
Patterns bloom in cosmic lace,
A dance of time, a timeless grace.

Orbits weave like threads of fate,
In the stillness, we meditate.
Each revolution, a story told,
A tapestry woven, bright and bold.

Infinite echoes in the boundless dark,
Whispers of creation, a constant spark.
Fractal dreams, a stunning array,
In patterns of infinite, we find our way.

Symmetry reigns in clusters bright,
A geometric wonder, pure delight.
Cosmic rhythms, a heartbeat so clear,
In the stillness of space, we draw near.

Each moment fleeting, yet held so tight,
In patterns of time, we seek the light.
And as the universe plays its tune,
We dance forever beneath the moon.

Beyond the Stars

Beyond the stars, where silence reigns,
We dare to dream, we break our chains.
Galaxies beckon with shimmering light,
Whispers of hope in the vastness of night.

In cosmic solitude, we find our peace,
A universe expanding, a sweet release.
In the arms of infinity, we glean the truth,
Beyond the stars, returns lost youth.

Wanderers at heart, we seek the vast,
Adventurers in time, shadows of the past.
Each twinkling beacon, a guiding hand,
Beyond the stars, our spirits stand.

Constellations tell of journeys grand,
Legends woven, like grains of sand.
In the breath of the cosmos, we feel alive,
Beyond the stars, we learn to thrive.

So reach for the heavens, let your heart soar,
For beyond the stars lies so much more.
In the dance of creation, forever we roam,
Beyond the stars, we always find home.

Reflections in Starlight

In the quiet night sky, the stars gleam,
Whispers of light, like distant dreams.
Each twinkle a story, old yet so bright,
Guiding our hearts with celestial light.

Mirroring hopes in the vast unknown,
They dance in the dark, never alone.
Each flicker a promise, a wish to be,
In starlit reflections, we find the key.

With every glance, a secret is spun,
Like threads of fate, they weave and run.
The universe speaking in colors and hues,
As we ponder our lives, our chances, our views.

Under this vast canopy, we stand small,
Yet feel the pulse that connects us all.
In the reflections, our stories unite,
Beneath the enchantment of starlight's bright.

So let dreams unfurl, let hopes take flight,
In the calm of the cosmos, we find our sight.
Reflections in starlight, our souls in tune,
Together, we'll shine, like the stars and the moon.

Celestial Puzzles

In the tapestry of space, constellations align,
Dancing in harmony, a puzzle divine.
Each star a piece in the cosmic game,
Whispers of wisdom with each fiery flame.

Mysterious paths that cross and entwine,
Mapping our fate in this grand design.
Galaxies swirl, their secrets concealed,
In the heart of the night, the puzzles revealed.

Through time and through ages, they beckon and call,
A riddle of stardust, binding us all.
In swirling nebulae, clues softly rest,
Inviting the dreamer to ponder their quest.

Cradled in space, we search for the thread,
Threads spun of starlight, the path that we've led.
Celestial puzzles, unweaving the night,
Seeking the truth in the cosmic light.

As we gaze upwards, our spirits ignite,
Deciphering the cosmos, embracing the night.
With each star we touch, a story unfolds,
In the dance of the heavens, the mystery holds.

Nebulae Dreams

In the cradle of night, where colors collide,
Nebulae whisper, secrets they hide.
Clouds of creation, in shades soft and bright,
Dreams of the cosmos, swirling in light.

Fragments of matter, where stars come to birth,
Ethereal gardens, adorned with their worth.
Each puff of gas, a celestial sigh,
Cascading the dreams that we hold up high.

As we wander through cosmos, our hearts align,
Kissed by the echoes of space and the divine.
In nebulae's arms, we find solace dear,
Floating on visions that shimmer so clear.

Starlight embraces the dreams that we weave,
In the fabric of time, there's much to believe.
Nebulae dreams, like wishes released,
In a dance of creation, our spirits find peace.

With every heartbeat, with every breath,
We're part of the cosmos, even in death.
In these vibrant clouds, our stories will soar,
In the ballet of dreams, we're forevermore.

Orbits of the Unseen

In the silence of space, the unseen does glide,
Orbits of wonder, with gravity tied.
Planets in shadows, they whisper and swirl,
Secrets that hide in the cosmic pearl.

Invisible forces, a dance without sound,
Through the galaxies vast, their paths are unbound.
Reaching out softly, they pull and they tug,
In the depths of the dark, like a warm, gentle hug.

While we gaze at the bright, at the visible sphere,
The orbits of unseen hold magic so near.
Silent companions, in darkness they spin,
Guiding our fates, the journey within.

With each passing moment, we drift and we sway,
Finding our place in the cosmic ballet.
Orbits of the unseen, a path we embrace,
In the heart of the night, we all share this space.

So let us explore, let our spirits take flight,
Trust in the unseen that dances in light.
Through cosmos and shadows, our spirits entwine,
In the orbits of unseen, forever we shine.

Luminescent Secrets of the Void

In the depths where shadows dwell,
Whispers of the cosmos swell.
Stars ignite in silent grace,
Hiding secrets in their space.

Galaxies spin in distant dance,
Echoing the void's romance.
Time and light intertwine free,
Unraveling mysteries we can't see.

Nebulas bloom in colors bright,
Painting the endless, quiet night.
Celestial tones, a grand ballet,
In night's embrace, they softly sway.

Comets trail with whispers bold,
Tales of journeys still untold.
In their wake, they leave a fire,
A flicker of the cosmic choir.

Eternal echoes softly ring,
In the void, the heart takes wing.
Listen close, the dark reveals,
A universe of timeless feels.

Petals of Stardust

Falling soft from skies above,
Each petal sings a tale of love.
Woven dreams in twilight's gleam,
Carried forth on whispers' stream.

Galaxies drift like fragrant blooms,
In the night, their beauty looms.
Sparkling dust on cosmic winds,
Nature's touch, the heart rescinds.

Every star, a wish unfurled,
Sown in the fabric of the world.
A journey sown in twilight's grace,
Petals fall, a gentle trace.

Celestial gardens bloom and sway,
In the dusk, they find their play.
Each glowing petal, a silent song,
Cradling dreams that drift along.

Embers fade but dreams will last,
Crafting futures from the past.
In each shimmer, a heartbeat finds,
The universe within our minds.

Cosmic Reflections Beneath a Pale Moon

Beneath the glow of the pale moon,
Stars reflect in the night's tune.
Whispers echo from afar,
Guiding dreams like a glowing star.

Silver beams on waters glide,
Where secrets of the cosmos hide.
In their depths, the stories bloom,
Carried forth in night's perfume.

Planets swirl in a silent dance,
Caught within a timeless trance.
Glimmers flicker in the still,
Awakening the heart's own will.

The moonlight bathes the world so bright,
Kissing shadows with its light.
In this realm of dreams and flight,
We find our peace in the night's delight.

Reflections bend like thoughts in flight,
Carrying whispers of the night.
Beneath the moon's embracing glow,
We discover what our souls must know.

A Journey Through Celestial Remnants

Past the edges of time and space,
In remnants where forgotten grace.
We drift through echoes of the past,
In a voyage built to forever last.

Fragments of stars illuminate the way,
Guiding hearts where wishes lay.
In cosmic trails, the old and new,
Each memory holds a vibrant hue.

Galactic winds whisper low,
Carrying tales of long ago.
Lost constellations in the mist,
Invite us to embrace each twist.

Through the celestial, we venture forth,
Discovering treasures of great worth.
A journey rich with colors bright,
In dreams of infinity, we take flight.

With every step, the stars align,
Painting pathways that intertwine.
In the remnants of the cosmic sea,
We find ourselves, wild and free.

www.ingramcontent.com/pod-product-compliance
Ingram Content Group UK Ltd.
Pitfield, Milton Keynes, MK11 3LW, UK
UKHW021348060225
4485UKWH00003B/20